MW01246068

by

Joan (J. P.) Miller

DORRANCE
PUBLISHING CO
EST. 1920
PITTSBURGH, PENNSYLVANIA 15238

Dorrance Publishing Co
585 Alpha Drive
Pittsburgh, PA 15238
Visit our website at *www.dorrancebookstore.com*

ISBN: 979-8-8852-7168-4
eISBN: 979-8-8852-7893-5

The
Pony

My brother and I looked over the table at each other and listened to Momma tell us Grandpa was coming this Saturday. Grandpa was coming! And, he was bringing the pony.

I'm twelve years old and my brother, Lee, is nine, and every year Grandmom Verna and Grandpa Reuben, who live in Kentucky, come to visit us. And every year, he calls us about three months before they arrive, and he describes the pony he's going to bring with him.

This year he's bringing a black and white girl pony, with big black eyes and a swishing tail. Grandpa said she loves children and will be a wonderful pony for us to ride around the yard.

He tells us that we'll have to wash her and dry her, and brush her, and feed her corn and hay.

Lee and I tell him that we'll do all those things and will love her forever.

Grandpa said her name is Poppy.

Momma looked at both of us and shook her head, then smiled. She asked us if we were finished with our eggs and bacon and if we wanted more toast.

We told her we were finished with breakfast, thanked her, and headed for the living room. There, we started talking about Grandpa's past ponies.

Four years ago, when Grandmom and Grandpa moved to Kentucky, Grandpa told us they were coming for a visit and he was bringing us a pony.

We were so happy we wrote down all the names we thought we'd name it, and cleared out a place for it in the barn. We used our allowance to buy some apples to give it treats, and some brushes so we could keep it clean and shiny.

Momma and Dad took us to the feed store and we bought a bag of corn, and a bale of hay and stored it in the pony's stall.

Each time Grandpa called, he described the pony and we got so excited we could hardly go to sleep at night.

That year, Grandpa said there was a shiny, red pony in the pasture, who pranced and ran so fast his mane flew in the wind and his tail flashed in the sun. He was a beautiful pony.

In the next pasture, there was a girl pony, who was small and had big eyes and bright white teeth. Often, the shiny, red pony ran along the fence and "neighed" loudly so the little girl pony would come over to his fence.

Watching them, it looked as though they were talking to each other and rubbing their noses together.

On the day Grandpa and Grandmom were ready to leave to come to our house, Grandpa went out to the pasture and called the shiny, red pony. He told him he was going to Texas and would be a new pony for two wonderful grandchildren.

All of a sudden, the shiny, red pony reared up and stomped his foot. He "neighed" loudly and shook his head and mane back and forth, and seemed very angry. Grandpa took a step back and looked at the shiny, red pony.

He looked over at the fence and saw that the little girl pony was standing there watching them.

Then Grandpa knew; the shiny, red pony loved the little girl pony and didn't want to go to Texas. He wanted to stay in Kentucky with the little girl pony.

That day when Grandmom and Grandpa arrived for their visit, we watched out the window and saw their car, but didn't see a pony trailer.

Sitting around the kitchen table and after Grandpa had a glass of milk and cookies with us, he told us about the shiny, red pony and how much he loved the tiny girl pony. And said, "I couldn't make him leave the tiny girl pony to bring him here."

"I knew that his heart would be broken and would miss her so much, I just couldn't do it. I know that you and Lee wouldn't want a sad and heartbroken pony, so I left him in Kentucky."

Lee and I looked at each other and said, "Oh yes, Grandpa. We want him to be happy with the little girl pony and we don't need a pony anyway. We have you and Grandmom here and that's all we need to make us happy."

THE PONY

The second year, that pony was a beautiful golden color and very, very strong. Living in Kentucky, he was treated very well, fed the proper foods, and was well-trained to do many helpful things.

Out in California, a state bordering on the Pacific Ocean, there were vast forest fires and the firemen needed strong, well-trained ponies to carry supplies up and down the hills to the firemen.

When Grandmom and Grandpa arrived for their visit, Lee and I were again at the window, and saw them get out of their car, but there was no horse trailer attached to it.

So as before, after Grandpa had his milk and cookies, we sat around the table with him and he told us about this heroic, beautiful, golden pony who went to California to help the firemen fight that horrible forest fire.

We agreed with all our heart that Grandpa made the right decision and that we didn't need that courageous pony.

The third year, Grandpa gave our pony to a little blind girl who lived next door to them. She didn't have any brothers and sisters and she was very sad and lonely.

The speckled black and white pony was small enough for her to easily mount it and get comfortable in the saddle.

The pony gave her a freedom she hadn't felt in a long time. She held the pony's reins and "clucked" her tongue, and the pony walked slowly around the pasture with little girl sitting on the saddle like a Queen on a Throne.

The wind was in her hair and the sun shone warmly on her face, and she was a very happy little girl.

Grandpa explained all this to us when he arrived and we agreed with him that he certainly did the right and kind thing, again.

So, my brother and I never got a pony.

This year's pony, Poppy, went on to become a "Police Special Pony," so we never saw her, either.

Our parents bought us a big dog, instead. We were okay with it, too.

We had fun waiting those many years for our pony and thinking of all the wonderful things we would do with it, but when Grandpa never showed up with it, we knew that that year's pony was a hero, and those decisions Grandpa made for us were the right things to do at the time.

I guess that's what we learned: Make the right decisions for the right and good reasons and we'll always be happy and content.

Grandmom, Grandpa and our ponies live in our hearts forever, for all the right reasons.

By Great-Grandmom J. P. Miller

December 25, 2019

CPSIA information can be obtained
at www.ICGtesting.com
Printed in the USA
LVHW080834190523
746880LV00017B/52